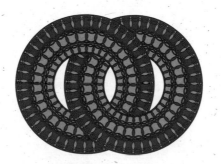

THRESHOLD

THRESHOLD

JOSEPH O. LEGASPI

CavanKerry ◈ Press LTD.

CavanKerry Press Ltd.
Fort Lee, New Jersey
www.cavankerrypress.org

Publisher's Cataloging-in-Publication
(Provided by Quality Books, Inc.)
    Legaspi, Joseph O., 1971- author.
        [Poems. Selections]
        Threshold / Joseph O. Legaspi.—First edition.
        pages cm—(Emerging voices)
        ISBN 978-1-933880-63-1

        1. Families—Poetry. 2. Homosexuality—Poetry.
    3. Poetry. I. Title. II. Series: Emerging voices
    series.

    PS3612.E3514A6 2017   811'.6
                    QBI17-826

Cover photograph credit: "Untitled, Sagada, 2012" by Frank Callaghan
(frankcallaghan.com)
Cover and interior text design by Ryan Scheife, Mayfly Design
First Edition 2017, Printed in the United States of America

CavanKerry Press is dedicated to springboarding the careers of previously unpublished, early, and mid-career poets by bringing to print two to three Emerging Voices annually. Manuscripts are selected from open submission; CavanKerry Press does not conduct competitions.

CavanKerry Press is grateful for the support it receives from the New Jersey State Council on the Arts.

Also by Joseph O. Legaspi

Imago (2007)
Subways (2013)
Aviary, Bestiary (2014)

To Matriarchy

Below the incandescent stars
below the incandescent fruit,
the strange experience of beauty;

—MARIANNE MOORE, "MARRIAGE"

Contents

xiii   Revelation

I.   Flower

3   Rouge

5   At the Movies with My Mother

6   My Sister's Wedding

7   Cockfight

8   Pigs

9   Am I Not?

11   To Whiteness

12   Peach House

13   Fingers, Hands, Hips, & Lips

15   The Last Christmas Party at Dr. Albert Elementary School

16   Dogs of Childhood

18   A Love Story

20   My Mother's Suitors

21   Imeldific

II.   Boys & Boys & Girls & Girls

25   Moose

26   Dear Echidna

27   Our Mothers

28   Boys

30   The Kisser's Handbook (The *Sensitive Male* Chapter)

32 At the Bridal Shop

33 [a subway ride]

34 In a Gully

35 Bleeding the Hen

36 Summer

37 Girls

39 Dispel the Angel

41 Hottie Sizzles

43 Marriage Sonnet (not based on a true marriage)

44 Night

45 Highway 15

46 Birthday

III.   A Book of Genesis

49 In This Bed

50 The Homosexual Book of Genesis

51 Whom You Love

53 This Town, Empty Nest

54 V-Neck T-Shirt Sonnet

55 Like Petals

56 30

59 My Father's First Birthday After His Death

60 Verlaine on the Lower East Side

61 They Say

62 Wedding Day

63 Chelsea Piers

64 Aubade with Excised Dogs

66 Triumvirate

69 Vows (for a gay wedding)

73 *Acknowledgments*

Revelation

Harper: . . . This is the very threshold of revelation sometimes.
You can see things . . . Do you see anything about me?

Prior: Yes.
   —Tony Kushner, *Angels in America: Millennium Approaches*

His moon-white torso flashes like strobe lights
in the club where we met last night as the subway stalls
on 42nd Street, *the crossroads of the world* sings the disembodied
voice of the morning conductor.
      I return to carnal acts performed
in darkness: kisses plump as crushed tomatoes,
my lover and I were ravenous, partaking on the harvest
of our nipples' rosy bulbs, tearing at our limbs like meats
on a medieval table. Our tongues snakecharmed goosebumps
to the surface of our flesh. His weight pressing
against me drove me ecstatic to asphyxiation.
He Anglosaxoned me, the divinity of his
England flooded my mouth with light.
      A conundrum this union
of identical bodies, fusing in hungry, irrational
ways, squeezing a camel through a needle's eye:
a defiance of nature, which is nature.
      I didn't know the man,
we were foreigners sharing a language
spoken incongruently—lilts, crests, pitches.
But I tread familiar territory like my childhood
tropics. I was sherpa to my terrains
of Asia, yes, the entire continent
for I had grown immense.
      At dawn, with his fingers the British
boy feathered the slope of my back,

the blue light softening his face,
and the world outside escaped.
        We entered a threshold of revelation,
ether of lucidity, truth-telling. I asked,

      When you look at me, what do you see?
      He said, *A homosexual.*

As he fell asleep, I watched the stranger,
the sour breathing of his gentle wellspring.
Where were the prophetic, wrathful angels?
        I then realized I am not afraid of men,
nor the masculine hyperbole of men who love men,
and my father was not in that hotel room.
        I felt the archipelagic islands had gathered—
a wholeness like Pangaea, when Earth was young,
its landmass unimaginably one.

I.

FLOWER

Rouge

My mother fishes out her seashell
compact. The rabbit tail brush dabbed
with pressed powder sweeps across my
face, feathering into alabaster, a masking.

Throughout my grade school performances—
whether stuffed inside a tomato costume or
sandwiched between cardboards to resemble
a book—my mother has applied foundation,
blush, talcum, highlighting mascara, to conceal
and reveal: boy and actor, flesh and porcelain.

Backstage, her slender finger glides her lipstick
red on my lips, pearly puckered. She's leaning so
close we're exchanging breaths. Transference
from a woman who never leaves the house
without her face impeccably drawn, hair
fashionably in a bun. Who, during the heat
of equatorial afternoons, locks her children
in her bedroom for *siesta* to preserve our light

skin. I am learning beauty, I am learning to be
feminine, and shoulder the cruelties accorded
a boy with flair. I put forth face of even tone,
void of harshness. What a beautiful mother
does to her son. Escorting him to the stage.

With the taste of petrolatum in my mouth,
hair slicked back with pomade, crowned
with a poinsettia headdress, I'm in the garden
of a Christmas pageant, perfumed, armored

with memorized rhyming lines and conspicuous
anonymity among bare-faced classmates. Before
a cat-eyed audience I flower, glowing in make-
shift health, rouge like smolder of the cheeks.

At the Movies with My Mother

Once again my mother and I have snuck out
to a movie theater, leaving behind my siblings
bruising themselves like ill-carted fruits on
a long journey and my father who remains

to be seen. In the dark and hush, we sit with
our hands greasy with the oil, sea salt, and garlic
of our fried peanuts while the flickering screen
casts larger lives animated by distant puppeteers.

We're stowaways aboard a ship, I'd fantasize
of our secret excursion (perhaps not so secret).
Or Pinocchio, in search of his kind papa, finds
him in the belly of Monstro the Whale. Rarely

do we watch a film I wanted. My mother favors
tearjerkers in which women suffer in martyrdom,
fall from high grace, seek revenge, and reap moral
redemption. In this communal, cavernous space

celluloid glow outlines each solitary audience,
embraced by air-conditioning, drowsing into
forgetfulness. I see my mother's eyes are fires
that could burn the unearthly core of a whale.

My Sister's Wedding

Her glass slippers fit. My sister
fairied around the waterlilied dance floor,

a floating replica of the
chalky ceramic bride on the wedding

cake, elegant with frosting,
her veil elongated into her train—

a frozen road leading
to its mountain.

She fussed over the magnolias,
settling her warm eyes on her men:

her brother snuggled fittingly into his
girlfriend, driving his tongue into

the pink internal of her mouth;
her father, nudged by his wife to dance

with his daughter, his bow tie removed
and a button missing from his shirt;

her husband, all perspiration and throat-
dryness said, *I'm going to miss my mother;*

and me, overhearing this, seeing all this,
sulked, sank, didn't tell her the signs.

Cockfight

The saying goes a Filipino man would starve
his family before he starves his rooster,

warrior animal, hope vessel. Bred and prized,
see how lovingly he fits a curved heel

blade bracelet over the gamecock's trimmed
spur, primordial legs scaly remnants

of its reptilian ancestry. Red crowns shorn
like dethroned kings in the humid arena

they charge head-on. Ancient lust rushes
up crested temples, hot-blooded waltz,

mirror in flowery aggression, ballooning
skirts of aerial wings, footwork knifing rapid-

fire blows, deep gashes. The men pump fists,
bruising what's before them, their mouths beaks

of a hundred downy pullets, shrieking like wives.

Pigs

From house to house, my sisters and I knocked
on our neighbors' doors and once let in we tiptoed
into their kitchens, or beyond, onto cement patios
where we emptied their tin cylinders of leftover foods

into plastic pails filling up with slop to feed our pigs.
Unlike clear water from a well, the stews stank
with syrupy, creamy mixtures of discarded meals:
sour rice, rotten fruits, foamy bread, fish gills.

At times, on our rounds, we encountered classmates
and slinked back in embarrassment. We never got
used to it. As with the rich homes we were allowed
in by maids who all looked like our aunts. Hit bottom

on the food chain. We began to resent the swine,
those faultless, omnivorous, gluttonous ungulates
in their domesticated, pink-eyed, curly-tailed splendor.
But when our mother called out her order, we obeyed—

we were respectful, fearful children—our schoolwork
could wait. We marched dizzily into the late afternoon
heat to collect again and again the refuse of human
consumption. In the fading light, echoes of porcine

squeals, we strained lifting our pails' mounting
weight. Inevitably, our arms buckled, the swill
sloshed, splattered over our hands, legs, whole
young lives, splashes of throwaway and waste.

Am I Not?

A boy trails a school of boys up a tree
for fruit-picking, or prehensile expedition.
He lags behind not because he is unskilled
at climbing, in fact, he possesses the gibbon-
grace of Filipino coconut boys in provinces.
      He trails to marvel at the twin jellyfish
of their underwearless shorts bobbing heavenward,
to glimpse at their flaccid nautilus, to bask
in their shared ocean life in the tree's ether.

                    >   >   >

Am I not that tremulous, salty-skinned boy
who trails like jet stream along bark and anxious leaves,
committing some thievery against the boys' oblivious
physicality and joy? I am stolen glances, surface
scratcher, light's glimmer, am I not? Anticipatory
and vigilant as a hatchling fish expulsed from its father's mouth?
I feed starry-eyed at the bottom
                                        Am I not your boy?
Who dangles from an offshoot branch, reaching for the plumpest
guava for my ripe mother? Sepal not calyx nor calendula.
Yet, too, am I not noncommittal substance like chalk,
pencil lead? I'm self-adhesives. Not your loose
tealeaf connoisseur scattering steeped, dried confetti
from windowsills for wind to carry? Am I an opossum
that raids trash bins, feasting on eggshells like shattered light?
The crescent moon that conceals? Reflection on the impenetrable
mirror? Am I no one's Promised Land, of distant adoration?
A boy better suited underwater, a dislocated tragic seahorse,
a darting, cautious sea anemone fish, am I not?

> > >

A boy visits the zoo, and weeps.
A hundred-year-old tortoise lives in a tank
no larger than its own body. It can only survive
this way, he reads tearfully, in the wild it digs itself
into a hole as protection from alligators, predators.
One of Darwin's fittest, the tortoise retracts snugly
encased in the carapace and plastron of its bony igloo.

To Whiteness

In the pale universe
of a hospital bed, my father
descends the depths of his dying.
His wife and children surround him
like a moat while the priest dangles his
rosary in prayer. With subterranean
calm, his doctor and nurses minister
syringes, dextrose channels, tubes;
the catheter lodged in his urethra;
conduits that feed and cleanse and
medicate the circuitry of my father's
cancer-ravaged, bloated, yellow body.

       The scene's stark whiteness,
of soft fluorescent lights,
of the befallen sacredness,
of respect for whatever is coming,
makes it difficult to hate a man.
Even my hard father who's been
plummeting from his drunken, stoic
graces for years. His cancer has struck
him powerful as the blows he'd laid upon
my mother, humiliating as the kick he once
bestowed my brother, a twelve-year-old
plunging head first into mud.

       Overhead hangs my father's
birthday banner on which I wrote *See
the lights*—a plea, a command, a wish—
for this bad blood. But my father
has lived his life as he knows how:
of selfishness, of absence, of solitude.
My mother squeezes his thick hand
as if grasping for something. Nearby
the white roses begin to curl in their water.

Peach House

My mother never wanted a rose garden.
What to do with a plot of land but dig?
Spade tilling sandy soil under the Southern
California sun, neon-green lawn emulating

Astroturf. It is the first and only house she
Owned, solely, her name on the deed while
My father slept away his American dream,
Which shriveled into a prune in his pocket.

I could pretend and speak of this peach
House, scented by lemon bushes, shaded
With fruit trees, as fulfillment of immigrant
Grit, toil and sacrifice. But mother did almost

Die when a pickup truck slammed head-
On, totaling her compact Toyota. Maybe
She knew, through the shards, that a house
Awaits if she returns from the other side.

Fingers, Hands, Hips, & Lips

Dainty like tines, fingers,
like teapot spouts pouring hot
shame into my parents' cup
of diminishing kindness.

Hands flourish, exclaiming the world's
festive beyond grief.

Hands on hips, feathering palms, akimbo,
right tilt of my sisters' conqueror stance.
Unsuitable for basketball, they curl
but never succumb into fists

—unlike my father's—

rather, lift the hips to horse-
rump pageant stomps.

Deliver lips into songs.
Piaf-sparrowing, Whitney karaoke.
High pitches & giggles & squeals

much to my parents' bursting discomfitures.

Yet fork tines spear the meat.
My María Clara graces fan the flames,
heavenly mock-diva tendencies.

Nonetheless: my disparaged humming body,

which father forces arms
to their sides, soldierly;
subdues into a boxed-in crate.

The stifling, as with

my verbose uppity mouth clamped
by mother's fleshy forceps.

Lips squeezed to fatty pucker
as if to extract a mollusk
from a conch shell.

The Last Christmas Party at Dr. Albert Elementary School

Sampaloc, Metro Manila, Philippines

The circulating disco ball landed
on his lap when the music abruptly
stopped. Which meant he was *It*,
and must walk into the middle
of the surrounding chairs of
cheering classmates, and gyrate.
Piston in a combustion engine—horsehead
pump plunging down an oil well—as our
teacher, obliging mistress of ceremony,
revived the thumping beats on the boom
box. No shy preamble, necessary persuasion,
readily he swayed, strutted, pivoted, kicked his legs up
to the hemisphere. We overflowed with Yuletide spirits,
high on parlor games as he spun long-limbed and golden
through the pulsating air. For a moment I regained
my lost self and noticed how his body had begun
its crossing over, the musculature exerting
a new tension of power, a sheen firmness,
yet retained an unblemished smoothness,
downy hairs. Sinews wearing the toil
of filial labor, arms tunneling into anthill
biceps. Upper back sloped down both sides, gliding
like sculpted lines of Roman marble onto a tapered
torso. Even his deltoids and gluteus maximus
had earned their scientific names. I wondered
at his early muscularity and passage into
inevitable full-blown beauty.
He danced, enthralled
by the blaring pop
song, his hips undulating
like a sidewinder, or
a deadlier reptile.

Dogs of Childhood

My next-door neighbor's dog
yips and barks incessantly
and I'm haunted by the dogs
from my childhood. Amos,
fudge mocha swirl, pink
lapping tongue of curious
affection, lived as shortly
as his tail chewed off
by a nursing sow. He leads
a litany of puppies born
in haphazard quarters
of our overstuffed
house in Manila
that died from early onset
of canine diseases, or trampled
by goats and cows in the chaotic
bestiary. The runaways surely
disappeared into bay-leaf-
and-peppercorn-garnished
plates, then into the stomachs
of vinegary men drinking
their salaries and livers
away. As boys we ran
in packs, fought feral dogs
with bamboo sticks, rusty
pipes, stones. We taunted
copulating pairs until the bitches
tightened and dragged their mates
like carcasses through cruel streets
that offered no mercy. Dogs unleashed
the lupine lust in us. As with the pup

my young brother let lovingly suckle
until its teeth nibbled his little nub,
suctioned, pricked, on fire.
He howled, bolted straight up
to running, the puppy dangling
between his legs like a rabbit's foot.

AH!

A Love Story

She was the most beautiful
hen, feathers the kilned brick
hue of New England autumn
before I knew autumn,
her radiating heat
the tropics of my childhood.
Summoned by her magnetic,
clucking love, I released her
from the coop, cyclone
of fowl drudgery, first
song of farm fandango.
Pubescent eyes met chicken
eyes electric between boy
and his bird. Her crown,
red as overripe strawberries,
flowered down to her
epiglottal wattles,
curtains of blood
suspended from her throat.
Then hand traveled the length
of her hen-ness—comb
to wingbow to shank—
compelled to explore under
her tail feathers, fanning
the pinkness
of the pudenda, puckering
like a mouth. What's a boy
to do, orally fixated as he
was, but press his finger in
against the bristling,
then moist suction,

swallow. Quickening,
his eggshell heart shattered,
his whirlwind self spun
like iron planets
orbiting below a cock
bellwether perched spur
and claw on a stormy rooftop.

My Mother's Suitors

The moment my mother tells me she'd fallen out of love
with my father, the Santa Ana winds still
for a wingbeat second and the lemon trees
shudder in the backyard, their fruits falling
in a singular hushed thud.
It is a quiet shaking. I sit across
from her at the kitchen table, a man
now, new to shaving. The knowledge
is no revelation to me, not a throbbing secret
made flesh, not a downy egg sac of spiders,
rather, for years, this lovelessness skulks
in our household like mice with bellies full of rice.
        How did I earn this disclosure, and why
after a slippery-fingered dinner of sweet pork sausages
and sliced tomatoes swimming in fish sauce?
The Santa Ana resumes its torturous blasting.
My mother then speaks of past suitors:
those who brought her gifts of rose water,
sugar cane, and summer melons; the jetsetters
who promised her the lavish gems of Kona
and Hong Kong; lovers who mastered the rhumba's
oceanic waves, the tempter's hipsway of the tango.
        It is astonishing what sustains a person,
what we live on, how my mother has blossomed
with age, as she savors her secret history.
I can't help but envision her by a window,
leaning into the night as her serenading suitors
gather below her, surrounded by *sampaguitas*,
luminous children in moonlight.

Imeldific

My mother wore a bun Imelda Marcos high.
In mod dresses, she strutted down crowded
streets, parting the Red Sea. Often in tow

was her son: a scrawny, sickly me, her most
beloved, loyal porter-boy. Both raven-haired
and prone to nostalgia, we made a curious pair.

Unless Buddha, my best friend, came around.
We loved watching my mother perform chores
in full regalia. Lipsticked, face powdered while

squatting down by the spigot with a pail of sudsy
water and a bar of blue laundry soap, her duster
dress a bouquet stream tucked between her legs

as she scrubbed away the world's dirt and grime.
Of a generation of Filipina women who idolized
a pageant queen, she lived for gloss and beauty,

believed in the armoring of butterfly shoulders.
Before and after the tasks at hand—the public
appearances at bazaars, schools, fish markets,

parading through shanties, along open sewers—
she worshipped at her vanity among fine brushes,
blushes, perfumes, rouge, hairsprays, and mascaras.

My mother painted her canvas, contouring the drama
of her face in the revelatory mirror as two boys glare.
Boys who will fashion themselves into womanhood.

II.

BOYS
& BOYS
&
GIRLS
& GIRLS

Moose

Moose are drawn to roadsides during rain,
explains Olga over breakfast at an artist colony in Vermont.
Sporting wide-rimmed bifocals—eyes dulled from reading
by kerosene light—she wears her dark hair parted in the middle,
pulled back tight in a bun, and her shirt sleeves rolled
up her arms. Again I find myself in the company of women.
The others are matronly, mostly mothers and grandmothers
from Midwestern states, and a Mormon college girl from Idaho,
all poets, oatmeal-replenished. Her friend Amanda once hit a moose,
Olga continues, on a miserable morning, such as today, in Minnesota,
the animal bolted out of the hazy greenery as if expelled from the kingdom
of ancient trees. She veered but time and space collided and she hit the beast,
her truck pounded into crushed metal, hissing steam mingling with
the drizzle. The moose vanished into the quivering spring thicket.
Shaken but unharmed, Amanda called for help. Olga and three other
women arrived, they searched at length, locating the young male dead.
They dragged, then tied the stag onto the pickup and drove off.
I imagine Olga in charge, draining the buck's blood, scooping
the viscera, the heart, her fingers between pancreas and liver,
her crawling inside the herbivore, hacking at the flesh,
dividing the venison five ways. I think: I'll write a poem
about this and Elizabeth Bishop would not be happy,
but like the moose, she is dead. When I look at Olga I see
her snip the scrotum with her knife, letting the sac dangle
between her teeth. What did it taste like?, the girl asks.
Meat, Olga shrugs, it tasted like pure meat.

Dear Echidna

My monotreme flower,
Claw & burrow into spiny
Bush, dear reclusive pop
Star of Papua New Guinea,
Upside down pineapple,
Prickly anteater that is not
Anteater, mammal-reptilian,
Beaked but no flightless
Bird, soft-shelled egg-
Bearing, leathery egg-
Rearing, egg-hatched
Puggle in warm pouch;
Nipple-less, lactating
Females of many suitors,
Promiscuous despite
Thinning existence;
Scaly males of the four-
Pronged penis, my
Funky cold medina,
Off the evolutionary
Tree, offspring of half-
Woman, half-snake
Mother of all Greek
Myth monsters, dear
Beautiful anomaly,
Dear unchanged, dear
Vestige of prehistory.

Our Mothers

Told us if we leaned too far out
the window the devil would push
us to our deaths, then drag us to hell.

Scold us for going to bed with wet hair:
nightmare fishes and blindness. Under
towels we hid, rubbing our heads afire.

Warned us against gorging on custard
apples or *duhat* plums or cotton fruits,
which gave us the runs every time.

Spanked us with their coarse palms,
broom handles and bamboo paddles
for our forgivable youthful trespasses.

Cursed us, therefore we learned how
to curse, blasphemy piercing through
our faint hearts, blossoming with fears.

Boys

There is no loneliness like theirs
Bearers of the burdens of legacy
Superheroes monsters Legos and blue
Boys are their mothers' true love
Prone to territorial pissing
Caterpillars between their legs
Drones boars and stallions
They tear small animals
Into pieces bound to set things
On fire wake-up in cold sweat
Castration and lupine nightmares
Boys look to the sky for escape
Fly dangerously close to the sun
Comic books spinning wheels a swim at sea
Boys kiss one another, and feel anger shame
Each slides a hand down the front of a woman
Continent in their imagination
Fail miserably there
Play the fool overcompensate
Spread out their legs to distant landscapes
Prodigal sons grow coarse
Rhinoceros skin a tusk while at it
Warring war cultures
Steel mortar plastic and wood
Pallbearers miners butchers and priests
Boys refuse to dance when the dancing matters
Destined to break their daughters' hearts
Their hair cascade like ribbons in barbershops
Mirroring eyes well up with clarity and remorse
Adam in the apple lodged in the throat
Prostate of the idyllic body

In search of their mothers boys will
Love many women and men
Musk oil the lot of their
Forefathers fathers
Mankind's foreskin

The Kisser's Handbook

(The Sensitive Male Chapter)

Awkward and dry is love.
A moist kiss simmers as cherry pie.

A peck reddens into poppy.
Several feed like birds in your hands.

The first kiss carries history. The customary roses,
a bouquet received by two.

On the right side of her mouth, she is your mother.
On the left side, she's the sister you never had.

If delicate yet firm, a kiss can resuscitate the drowned Ophelia;
hurried and open-mouthed, moths flutter out of her body.

A kiss that glides smoothly possesses the pleasant lightness of tea.
If it smudges, prepare yourself for children.

A kiss that roams the curving of the lips,
the tongue still tracing the slopes
even without her near is a poet's muse.

When bitten on the lower lip—*I am your peach*—
if she's left there biting, dangling, she'll burn the tree.

When she's sucking your lips as if through a straw
she wants you in her.

Never quite touching, sky and earth bridged
by clouds of breath, speak in recitation:
Because I am the ocean in which she cannot swim,
my lover turned into the sea.

Or cradle her in the cushions of your lips,
let her sleep in the pink.

At the Bridal Shop

The gowns and dresses hang
like fleece in their glaring
whiteness, sheepskin-softness,
the ruffled matrimonial love in which the brides-
in-waiting dance around, expectantly,
hummingbirds to tulips. I was dragged here:
David's Bridal, off the concrete-gray arterial
highways of a naval town. I sink into the flush
bachelors' couch, along with other men sprinkled
throughout the shop, as my friend and her female compatriots parade
taffeta dresses in monstrous shades of pastel—persimmons,
lilacs, periwinkles—the colors of weddings and religious
holidays. Trains drag on the floor, sleeves drape
like limp, pressed sheets of candied fruits,
ribbons fluttering pale leaves. I watch families
gathered together: the women, worshippers circling around
the smiling brides-to-be as if they were the anointed ones.
The men, in turn, submerge deeper into couches,
into slumber, while the haloed, veiled
women cannot subdue their joy, they flash
their winning smiles, and they are beautiful.

[a subway ride]

His artfully unkempt strawberry blond head sports
outsized headphones. Like a contemporary bust. Behold
the innocence of the freckles, ripe pout of cherry lips.
As if the mere sight of the world hurts him, he squints
greenly and applies saline drops. You dream him crying
over you. For the duration of a subway ride you fall
blindly in love. Until he exits. Or you exit, returning
home to the one you truly love. To ravish him.

In a Gully

A horse in a gully is not afraid. A child in a gully is. Lost, she's an ant twitching down sliding slopes. Hillside sediment, depression excavated by long gone waters. Did she fall; if so is she broken? How did she get there? Her wrists bend like sitting dogs, her knees are unpolished brown leather. And what of the horse in her dream, was it a dream? She hears the animal castanets of its trotting like pricks on her skin. Is that chewed grass she smells, the cud of safety? Hooves-clatter echoes like marching soldiers. The horse mystifies, its flanks are muscles of so much meat and the hair, the hair . . .

Bleeding the Hen

She's six and school has turned tiresome.
She storms home like a battering ram.

Her mother sits, serene as a water pitcher.
She drinks her up and bubbles inside.

Afternoon breeze, a spider spins its web,
catching little wings of island light.

Her mama's shadow, the girl will lengthen
immensely from backyard into life.

She crouches besides her mother, bleeding
a hen from its plucked sliced neck.

Red, warm on her fingers the woman draws
a cross on her daughter's forehead

as the hen convulses under the grip, fortifying
blood pooling at the girl's feet.

Summer

for Rita Zilberman

That summer morning you did what you have
never done: let go of your mother's hand.

In the open-air market, rushing bodies loom
like bursts of dark clouds or birds

of prey. Hands free, recoiled, your mother
springs into her wind-up task-making.

And you: drawn into, then drowned in a vibrant
rug's petal intricacies—its tapestry of green

branches, red clotted bulbs of dahlias—woven
in rural Russia, that simple fact escapes

you, yet inside your child-intricacies the Moldovan,
elusive as a native tiger, snow-dusted, stirs.

You recognize a self. As you witness your mother
shrinking towards a horizon. The rug hangs

like a garden, you are not lost in wilderness.

Girls

Are hemorrhaging
In waves of moon tides
In metronomic fashion
In the shedding physical
Renewal at the gestational center
Their mothers' right-hand man
Secondary in their fathers' eyes
Daughters shielded winged veiled
Far stronger than you are
Dolls dresses periwinkle teatime
Girls trash-talk & kiss
Pillow-lipped canary chanteuse
They can wreck your life like gambling
Debts like a runaway automobile with Mary
Magdalene pumping on the gas
Girls gust names of hurricanes
Muses of perpetuity
All fingernails & ponytails
Dun-colored peacock hen
Brides of ovary buds uterine blossoms
Nipple milk better-half
Homemakers secretaries & presidents
Gagged & pillaged
Hear me through oil and fire
Barrage their high threshold
Girls remain broken when unbroken
Sisters in hyena matriarchy
Their mothers are to be annihilated then cared for
Their children's hearts' left ventricles
Pills encased in pearly compact sundial
Womanly spine is the end of men

A love affair with is love for country
Penelope undoing the burial
Shroud Adam's dream Kali's fury
Messianic reproach burgeoning
Yolk girl furnace

Dispel the Angel

Lately his loneliness has sprouted wings.
It hovers above his darkened head like a desecrated
angel. It clouds his eyes with the cream of nostalgia.
It is the ghostly geyser of the spouting steam
when the kettle boils for his private tea.
In bed, balled up under the sheets,
an echoing cove of limbs, he thinks
of Orpheus: if only he could've contained
his forlorn love for Eurydice
and not turn back.
Such a gulf, sad bereavement.
Recently he's gotten into the habit
of talking to himself, at first in front
of the foggy mirror while shaving,
the blade scraping off lather to reveal
his translucent face, but now, often, he talks
in movie theaters, public gardens, on the corner
of Houston and Ludlow. At dinner, he discusses
Magritte and Hopper with his duck à l'orange.
The salt and pepper shakers can-can for him.
Later, he says to the lamp, *I haven't been touched
in weeks.* He senses he's transcended
the loneliness of the inanimate: of empty
corridors, of solitary light illuminating a house
on a stretch of highway in daytime,
of wet matches, rotting fruits, and dust.
On a summer's morning, he then dispels
the sullied angel from his shower, makes
an appointment at his neighborhood salon
where the shampoo girl will shiatsu his erogenous
scalp with her thin fingers. Soon after, on the subway,

sitting next to a man, their arms touch—heat traveling
by the wires of their hair—then rub slowly against one another
like the first friction of the earth.

Hottie Sizzles

for Ching-In

To you I am bacon,
sizzling on an iron skillet,
bubbling forth sexy meatiness,
strip after fatty strip of animal nitrate
juiciness, filling your dull existence.
I am your food of joy,
gastronomic rock-&-roll,
low-carbohydrates South
Beach diet. How you clamp
like a fat-o-meter, but I'm svelte
to a T, a runner's physique, yet unable
to outrun you. See these horse-riding hips
& flanks, if they were any more graceful
would belong to a stallion: Pegasus.
But let me revise these metaphors—
there are no cornflakes nor crumbs
in this meatloaf; I'm lamb
in mint sauce—rather here's an atlas
of my body: all smooth arches, steep
ridges, deep crevasse. Gluteus slopes
you can balance a Ming Dynasty vase on.
Lines plunge low on both sides of my torso.
& skin: twenty square feet of tactile heaven.
(I moisturize everyday & exfoliate
at least twice weekly.) & nipples:
soldiers saluting their high commander.
I set my faux-hawk Empire State high, head
of hair most men my junior pray & pay for.
Here are further revisions. An organic
metaphor: my arms are thickened vines.

Artful: I'm a painting of a haloed peach
hovering over a four-poster bed. Oh,
I doth protest too much. You hear
my body hum & want it only to burn.
At a luau. From charcoal & ashes
you unearth me, your roasted pig.

Marriage Sonnet (not based on a true marriage)

When he glares icily, you ignite like a lighter.
When he burns, you liquefy & stream.

You're salty margarita. He prefers martinis
with a lemon twist. Both : oblivion.

When away on business how you miss
your electric toothbrush more.

Why bring children to this lavish
party to never be invited again?

Matrimony was to save you.
Or even the field in a two-income economy.

If there's a heaven, he'd consider
goodness, which disproves your divinity.

Love is a lactating cow
plugged to an industrialized udder pump.

Night

When in love I melt into yellow,
blend in with every light to become
the most luminous apparition.

You've come disguised, hair
upswept, eyes two shades
murkier than petroleum,
a face I've never seen but know
in-the-gut-of-me, I seem born
from it, but in mirroring honesty

I often fancy you
are someone else, I prefer
this, realizing how lacking
you are, I can be happy
with a stranger moon.

Highway 15

The joshua trees are out there. We see them
when our rented car curves along Highway 15.
We have entered the Mojave Desert, *Like Moses,*
we chuckle, Catholics attending a Jesuit university,
proud of our impulsive act of setting out past midnight
through the darkness heading for the bright lights of Las Vegas.
                                    According to Indian folklore,
the joshuas are vessels for trapped souls—why the prayerful branches,
the sadness of the trees. We accelerate, northeast. The desert stretches.
Lights from scant houses speckle dozens of lonesome hamlets. Johnny
Cash croons on the radio as road signs fly past high above and our sides:
Apple Valley. Victorville. Calico Ghost Town. We're moving
20 mph above the speed limit. And the Earth is spinning.
                                    Meanwhile, the Crab Nebula
is exploding, expanding at the rate of 70 million miles a day, once
a supernova so bright it was visible in daylight. We cross
Devils Playground into Barstow, but before heading on to
Nevada we pit-stop in Baker, the Home of the World's Largest
Thermometer. 57 degrees at a gas station and 2 hours before dawn,
the blue mountains will appear to us then. For now, the sky is solid,
starry, and if a grain of rice is held up to it, I've been told, hundreds
of galaxies are contained in that magnified kernel of space. Back
inside the warm car that reeks of cheese fries bought at a local 7-Eleven,
our collective sigh hovers: our last college year and we are being hurled
into a future. At the tail end of the last decade of the 20th century.
Our car forging ahead, forging.

Birthday

I'm hiding from the doe-eyed mailman
with his Hallmark greeting cards, sincere
gift boxes, my mother's walnut brownies
and tokens of the zeitgeist. You see,
I'm a sophist, a writer and a liar.
My mother has never baked brownies
nor has she sent care packages laden with sweets
or salts. The phone is ringing, surely she's at the other end.
My answering is being debated as I speak.
As this poem exhales, second after fatalistic second,
like a fox fallen through thin ice, struggling to save
its dear life in the frozen lake.
I find the previous simile overtly dramatic.
No matter, for now the noon sun shines,
my curtains are drawn, I called in sick and imagine
my birthday cake ablaze in the office conference room.
How could a thing made of milk and sugar be so lonesome?
But there won't be cake. The cubicles offer no space
for such sweetness. I want to stay
in bed, fetal positioned under the blanket,
take an Ambien and sleep through the day,
knowing there are 364 more like it.
                        Let the mailman bang at my door;
let my mother question what I am doing with my life;
let the baker bleed and feed me chocolate cupcakes
with butter frosting. I'll perform a ritual: a blood-
letting of birds. Thirty species from an Adélie
penguin to a yellow-shafted flicker. A prick, a
drop, the ostrich dashes across the red savanna.
The kingfisher spears through green waters.
Into tree shadows the mockingbird
disappears, the beauty of all
my passing years.

III.

A BOOK
OF GENESIS

In This Bed

He sleeps. A solid man who could crush
me. Easily, if he chooses.

Barrel chest, curls frosted
at their winter tips. His neck's archer's

bow. Longing side by side, skins
white mineral, alien

almost, orbicular. Moist
still from benign meiosis. Suspended

capsules. Incubating hum. Soon we'd
rise like disenfranchised

souls to tend to bodily
matters, banal occasions. For now

in this warm bed we remain immaculate
yet ravaged, tarnished yet holy.

The Homosexual Book of Genesis

It is a short book.

God in His righteous glory conjures up
everything: the separation of Light

and Dark, firmaments, land and sea,
vegetation and beasts. On the sixth day

God, in His image, creates Adam
and Adam, sons of His patriarchal regime.

Then God rests. Then no begetting.
No litanies of descendants. Hence,

fatal rivalry between brothers, golden calf
worship and heavy rain are avoided. No exodus,

locusts, thorns, crucifixion and resurrection.
God rests absolutely, the seventh day eternal.

The serpent remains, coiled up a fruitless
tree. But as God's will, there calcified

in the larynxes of Adam and Adam: desire.

Whom You Love

Tell me whom you love, and I'll tell you who you are.
—CREOLE PROVERB

The man whose throat blossoms with spicy chocolates

Tempers my ways of flurrying

Is my inner recesses surfacing

Paints the bedroom blue because he wants to carry me to the skies

Pear eater in the orchard

Whitmanesque in his urges & urgencies

My Bear, the room turns orchestral

Crooked grin of ice cream persuasion

When I speak he bursts into seeds & religion

Poetry housed in a harmonica

Line dances with his awkward flair

Rare steaks, onion rings, Maker's on the rocks

Once-a-boy pilfering grenadine

Nebraska, Nebraska, Nebraska

Wicked at the door of happiness

At a longed-for distance remains sharply crystalline

Fragments, but by day's end assembled into joint narrative

Does not make me who I am, entirely

Heart like a fig, sliced

Peonies in a clear round vase, singing

A wisp, a gasp, sonorous stutter

Tuning fork deep in my belly, which is also a bell

Evening where there is no church but fire

Sparks, particles, chrysalis into memory

Moth, pod of enormous pleasure, fluttering about on a train

He knows I don't need saving & saves me anyhow

Our often-misunderstood kind of love is dangerous

Darling, fill my cup; the dove has come to roost

This Town, Empty Nest

There are no children here.
The adults are strangely erotic

in their miseries. This town,
wrecked, solemn, can be named

Longing: unplucked wild berries
dripping along infinite roadsides.

Longing dreams of honey-buttered
milled bread of a conjured city.

You, familiar with hunger, *Come here.*
You, with feral memories of wood

and stove and bed, on your leaving,
exhale the poetry of an immigrant

mother, the loneliest of beings.

V-Neck T-Shirt Sonnet

I love a white v-neck t-shirt
on you: two cotton strips racing
to a point they both arrived at: *there*
vigor barely contained, flaming hair,
collarless, fenced-in skin that shines.
Cool drop of hem, soft & lived-in,
so unlike my father, to bed you go,
flushed with fur in a rabbit's burrow
or nest for a flightless bird, brooding.
Let me be that endangered species,
huddled in the vessel of the inverted
triangle: gaped mouth of a great white
fish on the verge of striking, poised
to devour & feed on skin, on all.

Like Petals

Droplets of blood
dripped from the intimate bowels
spotted painterly, swirled
gauzily, flushed.

Earlier, when I cracked
the egg it dropped two
yolks like marigolds.

30

1.

I will publish a book by the time I'm 30.

2.

April, June, September, November.

3.

Breasts or chests and an empty stomach lying on their side.

4.

At age 30 my mother gave birth to me. Of five children, I'm the middle. Her favorite. The oldest son of my generation. I chose to not have offspring.

5.

I turned 30 on November 26, 2001. New York City still smelled of ash.

6.

An omen of blackbirds roosting on electrical wire.

7.

For the very first time I fell in love with a man.

8.

Every morning I count the almonds I drop in my oatmeal.

9.

There are 30 hours in a day, minus six, which I could totally use.

10.

Taylor Swift sings of young abandon in "22" (ooh-ooh). That I abandoned.

11.

I detest the rock band Thirty Seconds to Mars despite not having heard their music. Leto is forever Catalano to me.

12.

Space Station Expedition 30 Soyuz Capsule landed in Kazakhstan. A friend adopted a cherubic boy from a Kazakhstan orphanage. Renamed him Julien. He now resembles his French-Polish father.

13.

My sole brother's birthday is May 30. I often fail him.

14.

Forgiveness has proven to be the hardest lesson.

15.

Fifteen is halfway there. There is halfway to sixty.

16.

Adulthood prances nowhere near a New Yorker in his 30s.

17.

If I run on a treadmill for 30 minutes, I'll burn a cupcake. Or two.

18.

I met a lion-maned sorceress, wearing a glittery sweater. We ate dim sum. Went on adventures.

19.

The last TV show I regarded as religion was *30 Rock*.

20.

In many parts of the world 30 chickens constitute wealth.

21.

Zero Dark Thirty is military slang for the unspecified time in the early morning hours before dawn.

22.

"–30–" was the title of the final episode of the final season of *The Wire*.

23.

In *The Seasons of a Man's Life*, psychologist Daniel J. Levinson defines "The Dream"—youth, illusion, inspiration, omnipotence, heroic drama—and how it needs to be modulated during the transition period (28-33) of early adulthood. For survival.

24.

I aged out of "30 Under 30."

25.

At the end of a press release, the end of a story.

26.

In a clearing, a sawed-off tree. I count its rings. History.

27.

"–30–" was a telegraphic shorthand to "end transmission" in the American Civil War.

28.

My roommate and I rushed to our Manhattan rooftop and saw a tower downtown crumble into smoke and nothing.

29.

When my knee inadvertently touched his at a poetry reading, he moved not a muscle.

30.

Eyes inward, moan arising from the throat.

My Father's First Birthday After His Death

While I possessed the sentimentality of unloved children—
as with love, I believed death with its bag of tricks happens
to other people, dark smoke of mourning fumigating their houses—
I'm struck with prickly astonishment when I realized it is August 12,
my father's first birthday after his death. I step onto cracked pavement
and there he is steam rising from a manhole as if from an otherworldly
distance unfathomable, then he unfolds like a red carpet for a herd of
    thundering
wildebeests. How death plays tricks on you, this is Manhattan on a sultry
    late summer's
twilight. The traffic horse is married to the landscape, humidity kisses skin
    to perspiration.
Here's death's candor before me, celebrating: mice chewing the electric
    circuitry of a house
until it falls into darkness. Here's a day's strange fusion of birth and death,
    a collision
of a beginning and an end. Do I pray or blow ghost candles? With birth,
    life bursts
forth from a tear, it is bloody; with death life's ripped away, drainage of
    one's blood.
Birth comes painfully, expectantly; death holds no guarantees. This
    remembrance:
perhaps I loved my father—enough—to commemorate him . . . But death
    is no *ars poetica*,
writing is no transcendental match—measured, powerless, unequaled—
    this elegy dies here.

Verlaine on the Lower East Side

You: I am the fairer boy.

The Dionysian bartender punches in our separate cheques.

Fingers: licking sweat off my martini; yours, corseting rum & Coke.

A plastic beetle plunks from a fake tree. No stars just twinkling spackle.

We're netted warblers.

Let's exchange brochures, my computer interface acquaintance.

I do what you hope to find interesting; you do what I pray is magical.

Our tales twist like tongue-tricked cherry stems.

Face of a fox, heart of a dog.

Are you someone I would buy a bread box with?

This dialogue hopes for more: beyond social codes & rudimental mimicry.

Outside darkened, & taxis circling the thriving, heartbreaking avenues glow.

Corkscrew curl of lemon rind a Möbius strip suspended in vodka.

The twisting forks of my ribs are closing in on my beating liver.

They Say

You'll marry your mother.
But I, rather, my father.

Their prediction confirms nothing
short of presumption.

They loom, they rain,
pelting aphorisms.

Don't you want everything?
Have no room for everything.

Whatever happens happens for a reason
is but axiom of the season's predilection.

I love my mother.
I'm obliged to with my father.

Will I then end up with a husband
I shall out- and over-run?

Wedding Day

Best friends clamored to be
in our wedding portraits, pushing

both grooms to the ground.
We brushed ourselves off on the rusty

rings near the sculpture of the eyeless
bust, a giant chess bishop.

A field shouldn't be sedate but festive.
Trampled and citified.

Who amongst our gatherers kept
the fat-scraped shards of roasted

suckling? Who cruised
the manicured terrain, dragging along

slices of fruit pies? When the night
subsided there was more

than one union. We spun
like stiff children down a small hill,

faster and faster until we plateaued,
pulsating, purpling, aglow.

Chelsea Piers

My lover and I stroll down the piers,

post pescetarian dinner, in midsummer.

He points to the moon, veiled by clouds.

The Hudson River murmurs soft waves.

Across, the buildings glitter like theater.

Our arms damp, lamps lend themselves

to fantasy of the last two men on earth.

But as I reach for his hand, he pulls it

away, looks hurriedly around. Suddenly

I stand awash in brutal history, periphery

of sanctuary and danger. We are those

punished for our affections. The silent

seagulls disguised as larks. His denial

plunges silver-finned into the river.

Aubade with Excised Dogs

A landscape is not
complete without a three-
legged dog, I retorted, when,
in bed, he exclaimed how
we are in a perfect landscape,
buried volcanically under
a cumulus eiderdown, rising
like the Sierra Madre.
How we seemed to be
the same length, curved,
fetal, scissored, spooned,
we could stay horizontal
forever. What is time?
Is it a Sunday, Piercing
Light, indicating nothing?
While his booming laugh
at my absurdist whimsy
jolted another seismic
layer, let me remind
you, My Big Bang
love, of the many
mongrels that skipped,
sprung and pogo-sticked
into our sideline, they
appeared as if visions
from jungles, lagoons,
bogs and roadsides,
chunks of themselves
excised yet what's missing
completes, I'd behold them
foreground against backdrop

with astonishment, recognition,
in shantytowns, suburbs ...
As we lay, satiated in our
man-made environs, we
remember the pit bull
on a beach, oblivious,
unfeeling of loss,
jumping frenetically
as a wind-up springing
tripod. From its big
Cerberus head saliva
glistened like gossamer.

Triumvirate

1.

Raw, pungent heat rises from the bed, enticing the
moon into the room. We are made of everything and
nothing, of dark matter absorbing slivers of light.
We hum in masculine embrace. Bitten flesh, limber
limbs, necks, calves, crumpled white sheets, ears,
thighs, elbows on pillows, the mattress, spent. We lay
on a blanket of our twin bodies.

2.

With the moon still high I awoke to a half-empty
bed. Light from the living room frames the bedroom
door. I am dim and wonder, Is that my lover taciturn
with sleeplessness, his mind like ticker tape, trains of
endless headlines, his face computer screen blue? Or
is that my mother sitting up melancholy once again
with her clasped hands, her face the hanged pale
clock of the moon?

3.

Sharing a bed with an insomniac awakens the
latent insomniac in me. At last, I once thought, I've
abandoned my flock of sheep, starved for numbers
and fences, to pasture. But again I'm shepherding in
night's vast valleys, which somehow are less lonely. In
unison we toss and tussle under the summer moon.
Parched, we then share a glass of cold water in the
kitchen. At the table of our sleepless congress, he sits
with languid authority. I fall onto his lap, wrap my
arms around his torso like a marsupial as the hours
stretch towards blue.

Vows (for a gay wedding)

What was unforeseen is now a bird orbiting this field.

What wasn't a possibility is present in our arms.

It shall be and it begins with you.

Our often-misunderstood kind of love deems dangerous.
How it frightens and confounds and enrages.
How strange, unfamiliar.

Our love carries all those and the contrary.
It is most incandescent.

So, I vow to be brave.
Clear a path through jungles of shame and doubt and fear.
I'm done with silence. I proclaim.

It shall be and it sings from within.

Truly we are enraptured
With Whitmanesque urge and urgency.

I vow to love in all seasons.
When you're summer, I'm watermelon balled up in a sky-blue bowl.
When I'm autumn, you're foliage ablaze in New England.
When in winter, I am the tender scarf of warm mercies.
When in spring, you are the bourgeoning buds.

I vow to love you in all places.
High plains, prairies, hills and lowlands.
In our dream-laden bed,
Cradled in the nest

Of your neck.
Deep in the plum.

It shall be and it flows with you.

We'll leap over the waters and barbaric rooftops.

You embrace my resilient metropolis.
I adore your nourishing wilderness.

I vow to love you in primal ways.
I vow to love you in infinite forms.

In our separateness and composites.
To dust and stars and the ever after.

Intrepid travelers, lovers, and family
We have arrived.

Look. The bird has come home to roost.

Acknowledgments

A honeyed seedcake thanks to the editors and publishers of these fine print and online journals and publications in which the following works appeared:

Academy of American Poets' Poem-a-Day: "Whom You Love"
American Life in Poetry, Ted Kooser, editor: "At the Bridal Shop"
BLOOM: "Boys," "Fingers, Hands, Hips, & Lips"
Boog City: "Am I Not?," "Dear Echidna," "Triumvirate"
Cha: An Asian Literary Journal: "At the Movies with My Mother," "To
  Whiteness"
Codex Journal: "In This Bed"
Crab Orchard Review: "At the Bridal Shop"
diSorient 9: "Highway 15" (previously titled "Night Roads to Las Vegas")
The Drunken Boat: "Birthday" (previously titled "On Turning Thirty"),
  "Hottie Sizzles," "Moose," "My Father's First Birthday After His Death"
From the Fishouse: "Dispel the Angel," "The Homosexual Book of Genesis,"
  "The Kisser's Handbook (The *Sensitive Male* Chapter)"
Gay & Lesbian Review: "My Mother's Suitors"
HIV Here & Now Project: "Dispel the Angel"
The Journal: "Cockfight"
jubilat: "V-Neck T-Shirt Sonnet"
Memorious: "Our Mothers"
Newtown Literary: "They Say"
North American Review: "The Homosexual Book of Genesis"
The Oleander Review: "Dogs of Childhood"
Painted Bride Quarterly: "Pigs," "Rouge"
Pearl: "My Sister's Wedding"
Seneca Review: "The Kisser's Handbook (The *Sensitive Male* Chapter)"

The Shade Journal: "Like Petals," "Night"

South Dakota Review: "In a Gully," "Summer" (previously titled "Rita Zilberman")

Spoon River Poetry Review: "Revelation" (previously titled "Threshold of Revelation")

Tidal Basin Review: "This Town, Empty Nest"

Waxwing: "30," "Vows (for a gay wedding)"

Chapbooks

Aviary, Bestiary (Organic Weapon Arts, 2014): "A Love Story," "Am I Not?," "Birthday," "Boys," "Dear Echidna," "Dispel the Angel," "Fingers, Hands, Hips, & Lips," "Girls," "The Homosexual Book of Genesis," "Hottie Sizzles," "In This Bed," "The Kisser's Handbook (The *Sensitive Male* Chapter)," "Moose," "My Sister's Wedding," "Revelation" (previously titled "Threshold of Revelation"), "Triumvirate," "V-Neck T-Shirt Sonnet," "Verlaine on the Lower East Side" (previously titled "Rendezvous: Verlaine Bar, Lower East Side"), "Whom You Love"

Subways (Thrush Press, 2013): "[a subway ride]"

Anthologies

The Dead Animal Handbook: An Anthology of Contemporary Poetry. Cam Awkward-Rich and Sam Sax, eds. (University of Hell Press, Portland, OR, January 26, 2017): "Moose"

Kuwento: Lost Things (An Anthology of New Philippine Myths). Rachelle Cruz and Melissa Sipin, eds. (Carayan Press, San Francisco, CA, January 2015): "Fingers, Hands, Hips, & Lips"

Flicker and Spark: A Contemporary Queer Anthology of Spoken Word and Poetry. Regie Cabico and Brittany Fonte, eds. (Lowbrow Press, Minnesota, 2013): "[a subway ride]," "V-Neck T-Shirt Sonnet"

glitter tongue (https://glittertongue.wordpress.com/), an online collection of queer and trans love poems (2012): "V-Neck T-Shirt Sonnet"

Collective Brightness: LGBTIQ Poets on Faith, Religion and Spirituality.
Kevin Simmond, ed. (Sibling Rivalry Press, Little Rock, AR, 2011): "The
Homosexual Book of Genesis"

Soundtrack: M. Ward, *Transistor Radio*; PJ Harvey, *Stories from the City,
Stories from the Sea*; Lucinda Williams, *Lucinda Williams*; Nina Simone,
Anthology; Nick Drake, *Bryter Layter*; Fleetwood Mac, *Rumours*; Kate Bush,
The Sensual World; Joni Mitchell, *Blue*; Ryan Adams, *Gold*; Tori Amos, *Boys
for Pele*; Liz Phair, *Exile from Guyville*; Everything But the Girl, *Amplified
Heart*; Belle & Sebastian, *Tigermilk*; Cocteau Twins, *Blue Bell Knoll*; Josh
Rouse, *Nashville*; Michelle Shocked, *Arkansas Traveler*; M.I.A., *Arular*;
Sinead O'Connor, *Universal Mother*; Sade, *Lovers Rock*; Neil Young,
Harverst Moon; Dolly Parton, "I Will Always Love You"; Kelly Clarkson,
"My Life Would Suck Without You"; Rihanna, "We Found Love"

Blueberry mojitos on a golden rooftop for their friendships, generosities,
& feedback on this collection: Sarah Gambito, Idra Novey, Jon Pineda, &
Aimee Nezhukumatathil.

For cheerleader-like support & gastronomic company: January Gill
O'Neil, Jennifer Chang, Vikas Menon, Oliver de la Paz, Patrick Rosal,
Hossannah Asuncion, Lara Stapleton, Ricco Siasoco, R. A. Villanueva,
Nita Noveno, Marissa Aroy, Gina Apostol, R. Kristi Bernstein, Kay
Kojima, Joel Hoag, Ann Lien, Soo-mi Park, Karen Pittelman, Rita
Zilberman, Cecily Parks, Nida Sophasarun, Bino Realuyo, & Kron Vollmer.

For their good words, thank you Rigoberto González & Joan Larkin.

Thank you to everyone at CavanKerry Press, especially Joan Cusack
Handler, publisher extraordinaire, who believed in my poems.

Kundiman, Kundiman, Kundiman…

Manila, Los Angeles, New York, Nebraska…

All love, David Eric Rohlfing, my tiger, my bird, my bear.

CavanKerry's Mission

CavanKerry Press is committed to expanding the reach of poetry to a general readership by publishing poets whose works explore the emotional and psychological landscapes of everyday life.

Other Books in the Emerging Voices Series

Jesus Was a Homeboy, Kevin Carey

Eating Moors and Christians, Sandra M. Castillo

Esther, Pam Bernard

Love's Labors, Brent Newsom

Places I Was Dreaming, Loren Graham

Misery Islands, January Gill O'Neil

Spooky Action at a Distance, Howard Levy

door of thin skins, Shira Dentz

Where the Dead Are, Wanda S. Praisner

Darkening the Grass, Michael Miller

The One Fifteen to Penn Station, Kevin Carey

My Painted Warriors, Peggy Penn

Neighborhood Register, Marcus Jackson

Night Sessions, David S. Cho

Underlife, January Gill O'Neil

The Second Night of the Spirit, Bhisham Bherwani

Red Canoe: Love In Its Making, Joan Cusack Handler

WE AREN'T WHO WE ARE and this world isn't either, Christine Korfhage

Imago, Joseph O. Legaspi

Through a Gate of Trees, Susan Jackson

Against Which, Ross Gay

The Silence of Men, Richard Jeffrey Newman

The Disheveled Bed, Andrea Carter Brown

The Fork Without Hunger, Laurie Lamon

The Singers I Prefer, Christian Barter

Momentum, Catherine Doty

An Imperfect Lover, Georgianna Orsini

Soft Box, Celia Bland

Rattle, Eloise Bruce

Eye Level: Fifty Histories, Christopher Matthews

GlOrious, Joan Cusack Handler

The Palace of Ashes, Sherry Fairchok

Silk Elegy, Sondra Gash

So Close, Peggy Penn

Kazimierz Square, Karen Chase

A Day This Lit, Howard Levy

Threshold has been set in Adobe Caslon Pro, which is based on the original Caslon face cut by William Caslon from the eighteenth century, which was used in the first printing of the American Declaration of Independence.